The Things I Hide Inside

Devorae Huff

BookLeaf Publishing

India | USA | UK

Presentation by *BookLeaf Publishing*

Web: www.bookleafpub.com

E-mail: info@bookleafpub.com

ISBN : 9789357448116

First edition 2021

DEDICATION

I'd like to dedicate this book to my mother, she has always encouraged me and let me express myself how I needed to even if it was difficult for her to deal with. As well as encouraging me to follow my passions and never let anyone else tell me what to do with my life or convince me that what I want isn't achievable. She's the best person in my life and I will be forever grateful.

ACKNOWLEDGEMENT

I would like to acknowledge all of the teachers I've had over the years who have supported my love of writing and encouraged me to continue to pursue it and publish some pieces one day. As well as a thank you to all the people who said writing is hard to break into pick something else for pushing me to seek every opportunity to get my writing out there.

PREFACE

I have been writing poems ever since I can remember; and have even had some published in minor things for school or in email updates. I have a deep love for creative writing of all types but poetry holds a special place in my heart; it is where I turn to in times of great struggle as well as times of great joy. My hope is that everything I write connects with someone and shows that no one is truly alone.

Blue

I thought I was your comfort zone
A softer place to fall
When things were rough for you; was always
your first call
Could calm your soul with soothing touch, and
stop your thoughts from racing
What am I supposed to make of that now that
my heart is breaking
How could you say I meant so much and
whisper such sweet words
To one day take it all back with 7 words
It's hard to imagine it was real when your
feelings seem so separate; from the person I was
spent with
Now our interactions feel somewhat forced,
we're back to barely talking
Not sure how to go about mending what it hurts
to think about
Maybe one day pain will cease and being around
you will make me happy
We were a missed opportunity not meant for
solid landing
Perhaps another lifetime or a few years down the
road

We may be able to be again or feeling we'll
outgrow
Till then I set all things aside to have you in my
life; a piece of me you'll always have until the
end of time
Regardless of where we end up I hope we
remain, cuz being friends is better than living
with your ghost
To all the years ahead of us and stories left
untold; I will always love you, the girl who
didn't ghost

Should I Have Known

When you reached for my hand as if to hold it;
should I have known then to push it away
Sensed that initial interest would dwindle
That the flame of newness would quickly blow
out
Realized I was an idealized first romance that
turned bitter at the first sign of reality
Should you have picked another to save us both
time and energy
I guess I should've known to be nobody's first
and to not link up with friends
Could've avoided the heartbreak and this aching
hole in my chest
To watch you go on as if nothings wrong is more
than a little frustrating; three months I wasted on
you when you had no intent of staying
Another notch in someone's belt a distant
memory
I'd hoped you would be different, someone who
could love me
But alas mistakes were made and I'll take all the
credit

I was most at fault here for all that I expected
You're not ready for the long haul, I
miscalculated
It feels like lifetimes ago we were happy, a
joyful presence
Now memories of you bombard me with a
vengeance
Were there signs I should've seen that you would
soon be leaving, saved us both the trouble and
ran from all my feelings
Perhaps another lifetime or another world
entirely; we work the way I thought we would
and I wouldn't break down crying
Lasting feelings I'll always have but never meant
for showing, you were always meant for going
Love is a funny thing in the way it strips us
down, I'm used to playing the fool have always
played the clown
There'll always be a hole in my soul where yours
had quickly left me
A scar on my armor, I won't be show and telling
You're my past now and friends we will remain
Should I have refused to hold your hand and
saved myself the pain

Self - Inflicted Medicine

A burning sensation; coming from the depths of
a tattered, battered soul
An agonizing ripping allowing blood to flow
Unseen in a buried river beneath a porcelain
flesh
These scars don't mar outer beauty, they destroy
inner tissue
The heart stuttering and heaving, painfully
forcing out each beating
Last breaths are rapid inhalations barely
escaping slowly collapsing lungs
Life force slowly seeping out, eyes dulling in
color as light disappears
Body going limp as breathing weakens; falling
to the ground in graceful beauty
Soul slithering out to return home; body healing
slowly, returning to life
Not feeling any physical pain, when your insides
are dead and monsters overtake your head
Love pushes you deeper as feelings overwhelm
you

Till once again the ripping releases the crimson
river of pain; and all is momentarily weightless
and free again

Wind

It begins to blow hard and fast
My hair gets messy and windblown
I hear my name in every gust like a whisper
against my ear
The wind talks to me in different voices, but
sometimes the same
Sometimes it's laughter, sometimes it's tears,
sometimes there's screams
Always a constant reminder of what is and what
was
Sometimes I wonder if it's not the wind, if
something else is there
I sense something but still I see nothing, so I
continue on as if in a trance
Then the wind blows again and I find my way
back to where I belong

Rose

Red, soft as silk
Smells good enough to eat
Pretty as a picture, so serene and content
Hanging from a tree, thorns protruding from the
stems and trunk
Wilting, turning brown as they know the end is
near
Delicate little petals begin falling to the ground,
getting crushed
Then whole flowers begin to go missing, leaving
only a few
As the weather gets colder those to begin to die
Wilting away and falling to the ground
The tree waiting for spring when it can once
again start the cycle over

Hero

All of my life I sat up in this window inside a
castle to escape the torture for a little while
My father sold me to the duke as a slave to earn
money to buy more ale
The duke treats me well but longs to marry me
I have long golden hair that shines like the sun,
violet eyes, lips of pink
My name is Aurora Light
The master abuses me for refusal of his offer,
but I will not marry my captor
One day a handsome merchant happens upon me
and buys me
He releases me in the north but I stayed for love;
for finally making my own choice

Come Over

I see you staring at me from across the room
Your brown eyes sparkling with curiosity and
mischief
My breath catches in my throat anticipating,
then you turn away
Come over
I see you from my window playing with my
brother cause you live next door
Come over
As I watch you talking I wonder if you're talking
about me, you catch me staring and I blush; my
brother smiles, you run inside your house
Come over
I see you at a party, just as I'm about to leave
from the corner of my eye
I see you running after me, you grab me and
look into my eyes
Come over

One Last Kiss

Our relationship was good while it lasted but
now we must say goodbye
Cause I caught you sneaking around with her
going to all the places we used to go, laughing as
you did it
Does she know about me like I know about her;
will it kill her the same to hear my name
Do you think she's gonna stay once she figures
you out
When she leaves don't come around asking for
my forgiveness
You can't possibly really love me; but you can
blow me one last kiss

Why?

Why do we run from the things we want the
most; because the things we want the most scare
us the most
Why do we love that which only brings us pain
and heartache; because without the pain we
could not experience love
Why do we enjoy others mistakes; it reminds us
that everyone can be wrong
Why do we wish to fix broken things; we love to
make things better for other when we can't do
the same for ourselves
Why do we value money so strongly; it makes
us feel superior to be better off than people we
despise
Why is it so hard for us to trust; we withhold
trust because it gives others a power of us we
aren't sure they can be trusted with
Why do we fall in love; we fall in love because
we all need something to live for, to believe in,
to answer all the why's

Want You Back

You left in a hurry leaving no trace of you
anywhere
Breaking my heart and taking it on the road with
you
I tried to call you but your phone is unavailable
Facebook isn't working either
It's like you disappeared or never even existed
I don't see you at the usual place every week
I've told you I still liked you and you ignored me
I feel as though you hate me or just don't want to
see me
Why must you do this to me; keep in this place
I can't move on and I can't be with you; do you
enjoy this
I wish you could see that your life would be
better with me in it; I'd make you happier than
you've ever been
I want you back

Indecision

I don't know what to do about you
Every time I think I know, I second guess myself
Are you this, are you that?
How do I tell who you are inside, when the
outsides so confusing
You tell me this, you tell me that; then you do
something completely different
Have you ever been completely honest with me;
or is your idea of honesty dipped in lies and
deceit
My brain is swirling and twirling; so confused
I'm starting to blackout and now I almost don't
care
Whatever you say doesn't matter to me anymore;
I'm giving up on you and all this indecision

Wake Me Up

You left and it feels like I'm dying inside
My bodies ice cold and my heart has stopped
beating
Please tell me I'm dreaming and you're going to
wake me up
I awoke to find you gone and your stuff had
been packed up
I think I must be dreaming come wake me up
You left a note saying you'll be back for your
stuff
I sat there crying for about 2 hours until my eyes
dried up
Praying to god I was dreaming and that you'd
come wake me up
As my world was spiraling and coming down
around me; I swear I heard you calling my name
I tried to ignore it, but finally I gave in and
found myself in your arms
Thanking god it was a dream and you woke me
up

Confusing

All of these different feelings swirling around in
my head
Causing me to toss and turn while I'm sleeping
in my bed
I wish I knew which way to turn, but I feel as
though I'm turning in circles
When I think I know the answer the equation
changes
Leaving an endless swirl of answers running in
my head
A good nights sleep doesn't make me feel rested;
when I'm feeling so confused and twisted
Do I go this or that way, which way do I turn?
How do I know when i found the answer
Well I guess I'll just hope that when I do find it,
the answer will be obvious
I'll feel good and won't be confused anymore

Possible

Here we go again with these feelings; these
feelings of want and need for something I never
seem to find
A new guy with hazel eyes, curly hair and geeky
glasses
It feels like I have known him forever and have
just been catching up with an old friend; rather
than conversing with a stranger
There's something about him that's different,
though I am developing feeling; the normal
nerves are nonexistent
I feel safe and comfortable; as though I'm free to
be myself
Though does any of this matter, I've been down
this road before
It's a lonely path of rejection and pain, always
left alone
Why bother trying when fate seems decided on
me being doomed to fail
Though I don't hold on too much hope; I know
anything is possible

Monster

It comes and goes in phases like the waves of an
ocean
An ever present monster kept locked in a cage
that after much strain is broken
When the monster escapes he takes control like
a huge wave crashing on the shore
All things repressed begin to become the only
things you hear like screams in your ear
The feelings of worthlessness and pain become
too much to handle
Running for your secret stash of painkillers in
the form of sharp objects
Taking them to a hidden spot on your skin still
housing last times scars
Scraping and digging until the pain overrides the
emotions choking you from the inside
Till blood flows and the feelings get repressed,
you feel numb
Then hiding your stash and the evidence of a
resetting successful
Hating yourself for needing it so much; when
you went so long without it
The monster back in it's cage, mellow now until
it once again will break it's cage

Ode to You

This is an ode to the person I hope to meet
To the one who will put up with all my quirks
and insecurities
The one who will love me best in their t-shirt
and sweats; with pizza and a movie
They will accept that there are broken parts of
me that can't be fixed, no matter how hard they
try; and will love me anyway
To the person who understands that I'll stay up
late when I can't sleep; and allows me to be
grumpy in the morning
The one who understands sometimes I need to
be alone and that it has nothing to do with them
They will experience my anxiety and emotional
issues, and will love me and just hold me
through it
To the one who will give me treats and coffee to
brighten up my dark days
And celebrate the good times with our friends
appreciating how much effort it takes me
Who will understand my obsession with books
and constant need to write
They will enjoy my eclectic taste in movies and
music, as well as food

Will love my need to fill silences to stomp down
my anxiety
This is an ode to the person I hope to meet
If we ever find each other, I only hope that you
can love me even half as much as I know I'll
love you

Cutter

Paper cuts are like kisses brushing my fingertips
Eraser burns are like ribbons wrapping around
my arms
Lighters give me scars all around my waist
I hide all sharp objects, evidence cannot be
traced
My razors getting rusty but I dare not ask for
more
So I have to sneak around to get a number more
I wear long clothes to cover up my scars, that
wrap around my wrists, legs, and arms
An endless maze of cutting brands me an
outsider
So I go home and cut till I begin to bleed
Only my best friend and lover understands my
pleas
If only he was real and not helping me to bleed

Poison

I am the poison in my veins, the venom in my
mouth
The demons live inside me, of that I have no
doubt
Outside forces play a part, but the villain is
internal
Evil lives within us all, the void is all eternal
Darkness and despair will creep into your soul,
you will not recognize it's face but feel its
ethereal glow
We are the vileness in the world, our nature at its
basest
There is no good without evil, we cannot remain
complacent
The forever struggle of life remains the same,
whoever wins todays battle evil still we stay

Love Is Love

Why is it that certain people hate others for who
they love
Weren't all of us taught as kids that love is a
wonderful thing to be cherished
So why do people think it's ok to say that if you
love the same sex or a different race or religion
that it's wrong
Love doesn't judge or hate so why should we
Shouldn't we be happy for these people that
they've found what we all crave for
Besides just because you don't agree doesn't
mean you need to take it out on them
Love is blind, it doesn't see differences it only
sees what makes people compatible
Love brings together people who are meant to
make each other happy
We all want someone to love and accept us
But how can we expect to be loved and accepted
if we don't love and accept others
There's a simple phrase that sums up why we
should accept each other
Love Is Love, the sooner we except that the
sooner we can obtain it for ourselves

"Perfect Place"

There is a place in the universe where
everything is perfect and beauty rules
There is no hunger and all who live there have
riches aplenty
But this place holds a dark secret, and awful
secret
That for all its wickedness is what keeps this
place perfect
In a dark must basement chained and
malnourished lies a young boy
He is given no food and never allowed outside
He receives no kind touches or any form of
pleasure or affection
If he were to be embraced and brought out, the
perfection of the place would crumble
For their perfection stems out of this young boys
misery
Why you ask?
Well the reason is simple as any reason could
ever be
Perfection cannot exist without the misery's of
the world
So this boys life is sacrificed so their people can
live in peace and riches

His demise is what allows them all the worlds
pleasures
And as sad as it is and as angry as that may
make you
Take a second to think about the place in which
you live, in the society you call home
And tell me that we are not a member of this
"perfect place"

Monsters

The turth is monsters don't live under the bed.
Or inside our closets.
Or inside our heads.
No monsters are people just like you and me.
They live out in our world and do things like us.
They can walk, talk and act like us.
 They could be your best friend or sister or
brother.
They could be your father or mother.
Monsters aren't things you can see just by
looking, no monsters are only seen whenever
you're not looking.
They only come out when they won't be caught.
They only come out when they think you can't
see.
So while it's good to beware of monsters in
closets and under beds.
And even the ones stuck inside of our heads.
Remember they live in the world just like us.
But can only be seen once they've broken your
trust.